MW00474389

What Christians Should Know About...

How to Pray Effectively For Your Lost Loved Ones!

David Alsobrook

Sovereign World

ISBN: 1 85240 224 5

For a complete list of books by David Alsobrook, write to:
Sure Word Ministries, PO Box 2305, Brentwood, TN 37024-2305, USA.

This Sovereign World book is distributed in North America by
Renew Books, a ministry of Gospel Light, Ventura, California, USA.
For a free catalog of resources from Renew Books/Gospel Light,
please contact your Christian supplier or call 1-800-4-GOSPEL.

SOVEREIGN WORLD LIMITED
P.O. Box 777, Tonbridge, Kent TN11 0ZS, England.

Typeset and printed in the UK by Sussex Litho Ltd, Chichester, West Sussex.

Contents

3

Preface

Every Christian prays for the salvation of the lost. (It's instinctive to our new nature to do this.) It may be a lost friend, a lost neighbor, lost associates at the workplace, or for the lost in countries who have never heard the Gospel. Most likely it is for all I have already mentioned plus many more. We pray for the salvation of the lost in our society, for our leaders on the political scene, for our children's playmates, and others. This is because every believer partakes of the *agape love* of God which is extended, John 3:16 says, to "the sons of Adam" (the literal Greek for "world"). The love of God within us projects out of our hearts toward the lost around us.

But every believer I know, and I know many, will tell you what type of lost person they pray for most – their lost loved ones. The salvation of our families is the dearest thing to our hearts. We long for our loved ones in both our immediate and extended families to come to know the joy of Christ's forgiveness in their hearts.

Everyone prays for their lost loved ones, but this book focuses on how to pray **effectively** for them. I have been teaching this message approximately twenty years and first published it in a booklet called *And Thy*

House almost seventeen years ago. The results have been dramatic. Three hundred thousand (300,000) copies of *And Thy House* have been distributed in many parts of the world. Oftentimes one copy of this booklet has been passed around to many believers becoming ragged and worn with use. The prayer in the back of the booklet has been photocopied and distributed to entire communities of believers who have put in the names of their lost loved ones and prayed fervently for their salvation. Christian presses in different parts of the world have asked permission to translate and publish this booklet so the believers in their countries could come to a fuller understanding of these truths. Only God knows how many thousands of His people have read *And Thy House* and how many souls have come to Him as a result.

Over the course of these last seventeen years I have received literally **hundreds** of heartwarming letters from grateful readers whose husbands, wives, sons, daughters, brothers, sisters, grandparents, aunts, uncles, and cousins have come to the Lord **within days or weeks** of applying the truths in *And Thy House*, and praying the prayer in the back.

Most recently I was speaking at the final service of a series of meetings we were conducting in the Seattle, Washington area (I am an evangelist and itinerant Bible teacher). The exact date was February 9, 1998. As I was praying with people on an individual basis a dear little lady came running up to me in tears. "Are you the writer of *And Thy House*?" she asked excitedly. I replied that I was and she grabbed me with both arms squeezing me with all her might. Then she told me, and all the congregation at Faith and Vision Ministries, how she had received this book through a famous television evangelist who had recently published it.

"Within eight days," she wept, "my son, 38 years of age, came to the Lord while alone in his room. He was in a psychiatric hospital where he was being unsuccessfully treated for complete dysfunction. He has never been able to keep a job for any time at all or maintain any type of personal relationship with anyone. But after I got your book I put his name in the back and interceded for his salvation. I knew the Lord was moving for my son. Eight days later it was as though the Lord came into his room, touched his mind, saved his soul, and completely changed him. His doctors were amazed. He was soon released from care, moved into his own place, got and kept a job all these months, and loves everyone. He is a brand new person!" By this time all of us were rejoicing with her. (You can verify her story with Pastors Jack and Sue Bernard, Auburn, Washington.) We have probably seen more people saved through *And Thy House* than through our evangelistic meetings.

It is with great joy and anticipation of thousands of more souls that I now release *How To Pray **Effectively** For Your Lost Loved Ones*. It is a complete revision of *And Thy House* containing all the pertinent information of the former booklet, with additional revelation which has come to us over these many years.

This book will help you pray effectively for your family members who do not, as yet, know our Lord. There is tremendous power in fervent, faith-filled prayer! And, as you will see in these pages, there is a special guarantee for the salvation of your lost loved ones. The biblical truths contained in this book will

show you how your loved ones can and will be saved!
    Be of good cheer!

Evangelist David Alsobrook
Nashville, Tennessee
March 19, 1998

Sure Word Ministries,
PO Box 2305,
Brentwood, TN
37024-2305, USA

1

God's Guarantee

Is there a guarantee in God's Word to save your loved ones? After years of careful research I believe the answer is **yes!** In the voyage of life God has promised to give *"all who sail with you."* (Acts 27:24)

Consider the following texts which, I believe, will show you clearly God's promises of household salvation:

The Promise of Salvation for Your Children

There are abundant promises in the Word of God for your children's salvation. Prayerfully read the following verses and note carefully what the Lord has promised for your sons and daughters.

The Promise of Their Well-Being

> *And all your sons will be taught of the Lord; and the well-being of your sons will be great.*
>   (Isaiah 54:13 NASB)

*All your children **shall be** taught by the LORD,*
*And great **shall be** the peace of your children.*
(Isaiah 54:13)

The Promise of Their Return to God's Ways

Thus says the LORD:

"Refrain your voice from weeping,
And your eyes from tears;
For your work shall be rewarded, says the LORD,
And they shall come back from the land of the enemy.
There is hope in your future, says the LORD,
That your children shall come back to their own border." (Jeremiah 31:16, 17)

Train up a child in the way he should go,
And when he is old he will not depart from it.
(Proverbs 22:6)

The Promise of Household Salvation

*Then Peter said to them, "Repent, and let every one of you be baptized in the name of Jesus Christ for the remission of sins; and you shall receive the gift of the Holy Spirit. For the promise is to you **and to your children**, and to all who are afar off, as many as the Lord our God will call."* (Acts 2:39)

So they said, "Believe on the Lord Jesus Christ,

and you will be saved, you and your household."
...and he rejoiced, having believed in God with all
his household.   (Acts 16:31, 34)

This promise was prefigured in the Old Testament. During the first Passover each head of a Hebrew household took the blood from one lamb and sprinkled its blood over the doorway of his home, while his family abode inside the house. Moses had previously instructed the nation: *"On the tenth of this month every man shall take himself a lamb, according to the house of his father, **a lamb for a household**."* (Exodus 12:3) One lamb covered an entire family. Jesus, our Passover lamb, has been sacrificed for us. He is the Passover! He is the lamb for a household! (*see* 1 Corinthians 5:7)

The Promise of Salvation for Your Grandchildren:

The children of your servants will continue,
And their descendants will be established before
You.   (Psalm 102:28)

"As for Me," says the LORD, "this is My covenant with them: My Spirit who is upon you, and My words which I have put in your mouth, shall not depart from your mouth, nor from the mouth of your descendants, nor from the mouth of your descendants' descendants," says the LORD, "from this time and forevermore."   (Isaiah 59:21)

There are two distinct theological camps when it

comes to soteriology (the doctrines of saving grace): Calvinism (better termed Reformed theology) and Arminianism. Regardless of your personal convictions in either camp, let me assure you that you can pray with confidence for the salvation of your loved ones for the following reasons.

The Arminian may object to the concept of household salvation on the grounds that it seems to violate the free will of the lost. I have studied free moral agency at great lengths in the Scripture and believe that Adam possessed this faculty prior to his willful sin, but when he fell, or more accurately jumped into the ditch of sin (as it did not happen accidentally), his understanding became darkened and his will became subject to sin. The lost are not free, Jesus said, but are rather slaves, and will not, apart from the influences of grace, come to the light that they might be saved. (*see* John 5:40; 8:34) The Arminian can claim the salvation of his lost loved ones in the confidence that light is stronger than darkness and that no one in his right mind, free from satanic influence, would reject the light of Christ.

The Calvinist may dispute household salvation with the argument that no one knows whom God has or has not elected unto salvation. Jonathan Edwards, a preeminent Calvinist, is widely known to have believed in generational grace (this was part of Edwards' covenant theology). Indeed, his direct descendants, to this very day, are practicing Christians. Evidently, Edwards saw no contradiction between election and household salvation. A Calvinist can approach this subject with the understanding that God, in His all-seeing wisdom, may have elected the descendants of a believer to faith (especially since He said *"the promise is unto your children"*), and since no one knows who is or who is not chosen unto salvation, a believer may, upon the grounds of Scripture, claim the salvation of his offspring in the hope that they are elected.

So, dear reader, whether you are Arminian or Calvinistic in your soteriology, please read on! It doesn't matter how resistant your loved ones may be to the good news, nor how long they have hardened themselves against the conviction of the Holy Spirit. God is a covenant-keeping God, and salvation is a covenant that extends beyond an individual believer to include the entire family.

The Promise for Your Spouse

Believers are encouraged to marry believers. *"Do not be unequally yoked together with unbelievers."* (2 Corinthians 6:14) When a believer purposely marries an unbeliever Paul asks, *"For how do you know, O wife, whether you will save your husband? Or how do you know, O husband, whether you will save your wife?"* (1 Corinthians 7:16) Any believer who purposely marries an unbeliever is taking a big risk. Nevertheless, there are specific promises for those who come to faith in Christ after marriage, but whose spouses yet remain in unbelief.

> *For the unbelieving husband is sanctified by the wife, and the unbelieving wife is sanctified by the husband; otherwise your children would be unclean, but now they are holy.* (1 Corinthians 7:14)

What is meant by the phrase "the unbelieving (spouse) is sanctified by the (believing spouse)"? It must mean that the unbelieving spouse is the unknowing recipient of divine grace due to the special position of favor given to the believing partner. The New Geneva Study Bible comments:

> *Even the spouse who refuses to believe comes under the influence of God's work – much more so the children who are not old enough to profess their faith.* (page 1807)

This, in itself, does not unconditionally guarantee the salvation of a lost mate, but it does promise that the influences of grace will extend to that individual, gently opening his or her stubborn heart to the effective persuasion of the Spirit. (We will study, in the pages that follow, why the lost stay lost and what believers can do about it through intercession to God and warfare against the enemy.)

Peter advises Christian wives to win their unsaved husbands to the Lord "without a word" (without preaching to them) by living out the new life of Christ before their husbands:

> *Wives, likewise, be submissive to your own husbands, that even if some do not obey the word, they, without a word, may be won by the conduct of their wives, when they observe your chaste conduct accompanied by fear.* (1 Peter 3:1)

The promises for spousal salvation are not as emphatic nor as clearly outlined in the Scriptures as those promises for the children of believing parents. I ask, in response, what do Christian husbands and wives have to lose if they stand in the gap for their unsaved mates? The answer is simple. Nothing. (If their unsaved partners die in their sins they will perish anyway.) What do they have to win if they stand in the gap for their unsaved mates? Everything. (If their unsaved partners come to faith in Christ they will possess eternal life.)

What harm can there possibly be in a believer standing in the gap for his or her spouse?

The only logical answer is that there can be no possible harm.

Disappointment cannot be reason enough not to encourage believers to believe for their mates since, if their spouses die in unbelief they will perish anyway. Wouldn't that still bring disappointment since no believer could be happy over the death of an unbelieving spouse? Doesn't every Christian who is married to an unchristian have deep within the soul an abiding passion for the salvation of his or her mate? Of course! **Again, what harm can there possibly be in a believer standing in the gap for his or her spouse?**

I repeat: the only logical answer is that there can be no possible harm, while, on the other hand, there can be possible blessing – far greater than if the believing spouse does not take an active role in the salvation of his lost loved one. Remember, after all, that it was to a husband and a father that Paul and Silas promised his entire family's salvation, and also call to mind the many Scriptures which teach that God is no respecter of persons, especially persons of faith:

So they said, "Believe on the Lord Jesus Christ,

and you will be saved, you and your household."
...and he rejoiced, having believed in God with all
his household.   (Acts 16:31, 34)

2

How To Intercede For Your Lost Loved Ones

And it came to pass, when God destroyed the cities of the plain, that God remembered Abraham and sent Lot out of the midst of the overthrow, when He overthrew the cities in which Lot had dwelt.

(Genesis 19:29)

Three times in the Scriptures we read of the special relationship Abraham enjoyed with the Lord designated by the phrase "the friend of God." (*see* 2 Chronicles 20:7; Isaiah 41:8; James 2:23)

As God's friend, Abraham occupied a position of preferred favor with God by virtue of a covenant the Lord had made with him. Abraham was showered with blessing upon blessing as he walked in covenantal relationship with Yahweh. At the beginning of this relationship the Lord told Abraham to leave Ur, the land of his father and his relatives, and go to a land that Yahweh would give him to inherit. (*see* Genesis 12:1-9) Abraham obeyed the voice of the Lord and departed from Ur, but did not leave all his relatives. He brought his nephew, Lot, with him.

Abraham had two brothers: Nahor and Haran. Scholars suggest that Abraham took Haran's son, Lot, with him when he left Ur because Haran had already died and Abraham became the replacement father figure in his nephew's life. (*see* Genesis 11:28) Perhaps Abraham, or Abram as he was known at that time, and his wife, Sarai, felt strong parental ties with their nephew (since they were childless). Whatever his reasons for bringing Lot, Abram evidently did not feel it was a violation of the Lord's command. What we do know for certain is that Lot caused Abraham a "lot" of problems!

On one occasion Abraham had to rescue Lot from a confederacy of kings who had kidnapped him during an attack on Sodom. (*see* Genesis 14:1-24) Earlier Lot's shepherds had caused strife with Abraham's men, and, when offered his choice of Abraham's land, Lot had selfishly chosen the most fertile area, leaving the arid land for his generous uncle! (*see* Genesis 13:10, 11)

It was his very choice of this land, motivated by greed, which resulted in Lot and his family eventually moving to Sodom, a most corrupt city. Lot, a successful businessman, became a respected and influential elder in this city, but his influence for the Lord was pitifully weak, not only among the town's residents, but even among his own family. So non-existent was his spiritual leadership in his home that his future sons-in-law thought Lot was joking when he tried to warn them of the impending judgment which was to befall Sodom. (*see* Genesis 19:14) In fact, Lot's daughters, immediately after they were rescued from Sodom, induced their father to drink too much wine on two successive evenings in order to get him to commit incest with each of them so they could bear children! Evidently, his daughters failed to appreciate the error of their ways, but the products of their incest, Ammon and

Moab, certainly did.

Lot's spiritual influence was nil! Even his wife looked back longingly at her possessions which were going up in smoke and was crystallized for her disobedience to the angels' command. (*see* Genesis 19:17, 26) To his credit, Lot was vexed by the filth he saw all around him in Sodom, Peter tells us, which shows that Lot himself was not totally reprobate or corrupt, but the fact remains that he had chosen to live in a large commercial area where he could get a better price for his livestock, all the while subjecting his soul and his family's morals to the gross evil in that perverted society, rather than separate himself from that area like his uncle did. (*see* 2 Peter 2:8) Lot was not an uncompromisingly righteous person, which is inferred in our opening text, for when God destroyed Lot's chosen city He did not deliver Lot based upon his own relationship with God, but rather because his uncle, Abraham, knew the Lord in a special way and had obviously interceded for Lot. It is unthinkable that Abraham cared about Sodom. Indeed Lot and his family were the motive behind Abraham's intercessory petition in Genesis 18. It was because of Abraham's prayers and relationship with Yahweh that Lot was spared. Notice how the inspired record states it: *God remembered Abraham and sent Lot out!*

Lot was spared the destruction of the other inhabitants of Sodom because of his uncle's relationship with God. The Lord brought Lot out of Sodom, sending His angels to take him, his wife and his daughters by the hand and literally draw them out of that wicked city before the brimstone fell upon it. God did all of this as a favor for his friend, Abraham, just like you would help a friend who came to you asking you to help someone else on your friend's behalf.

This is the essence of intercession. An intercessor is one who is in right relationship with God and who stands before the Lord on behalf of an individual for whom he is concerned. He serves the individual by priestly service offering the sacrifice of Jesus' blood for the merit of this unworthy person who desperately needs the grace of God showered upon his life. The person for whom the intercessor is praying is not an individual who has an unblemished record. Quite the opposite. Yet, God moves upon that unworthy person in answer to the prayers of one of His chosen servants – the one who is himself righteous through the gift of grace. Notice how an obscure verse in Job states this truth:

> *He will even deliver the one [for whom you intercede] who is not innocent: yes, he will be delivered through the cleanness of your hands.*
>
> (Job 22:30 AMP)

Was this not the case with Abraham and Lot? You might answer in the affirmative but then object on the grounds that you are not Abraham. This is true. You are not Abraham. **You are Abraham's seed!**

> *And if you are Christ's, then you are Abraham's seed, and heirs according to the promise.*
>
> (Galatians 3:29)

The believer is an offspring of Abraham and an heir to all the promises God gave him. By comparison, you may have a nephew or a son out in the world, but God remembers you, dear friend, and will send your "Lot" out before destruction falls!

Prior to the destruction of Sodom we read of Abraham's intercession for that city due to the fact that he knew his nephew and family lived there. (*see* Genesis 18:16-33) He entreated the Lord to spare Sodom if fifty righteous persons were found in it. Sodom was a large ancient city, yet God promised to spare it if only fifty righteous were found in it. Abraham knew the reputation of Sodom, so he besought the Lord to spare it if only forty-five righteous were found. The Lord promised to spare it for the sake of forty-five righteous persons. With deep reverence Abraham got the number down to ten. It little mattered anyway because Lot and his family, four persons, had not even influenced six other persons for righteousness, so lacking was their own spiritual development.

What did godly Abraham do? *"And Abraham went early in the morning to the place where he had stood before the LORD."* (*see* Genesis 19:27) From this vantage point he surveyed all the land of Sodom before him, which was now billowing forth pillars of smoke as a result of the fire and brimstone which God had rained upon the area. In his heart he may have wondered about his nephew, the one for whom he had constantly prayed since his previous meeting with God on this very site, where he had besought the Lord to spare Sodom for the sake of ten righteous persons. Abraham wondered how Lot had fared. It was probably sometime later before Lot, now bereft of all possessions but his life, was able to get word to his uncle of the Lord's mercy. Lot had been saved, *"yet so as by fire."* Still, he had been saved!

(*see* 1 Corinthians 3:15)

In the final analysis of this inspired account we must conclude that God delivered the one for whom Abraham interceded, even though he was not innocent of the causes which brought him into the dire place where he faced destruction. Lot (and his family) was delivered from the fiery doom everyone else experienced, and all of this was due to the cleanness of his intercessor's hands.

Through intercessory prayer for our lost loved ones we stand in the gap for them and make up the hedge they are lacking. (*see* Ezekiel 22:30) God loves intercessors! They hold a dear place in His heart. He even promised them special protection in Ezekiel 9:4.

Intercessors are, in reality, new covenant priests who go to God on behalf of those for whom the Spirit burdens them, and present the needs of others, asking for God's favor by virtue of Christ's all-sufficient sacrifice. Every believer has the privilege of priestly ministry:

> *But you are a chosen generation,* ***a royal priesthood****, a holy nation, His own special people that you may proclaim the praises of Him who called you out of darkness into His marvelous light.*
> (1 Peter 2:9)

Not only are we, as believers, **priests** unto God, we have also been made **kings**:

> *To Him who loved us and washed us from our sins in His own blood, and* ***has made us kings and***

priests to His God and Father, to Him be glory and dominion forever and ever. Amen.
(Revelation 1:5e, 6)

As priests we have the **responsibility** to offer spiritual sacrifices. As kings we have the **privilege** of reigning in this present life and ruling over our enemies:

*...you also, as living stones, are being built up a spiritual house, **a holy priesthood, to offer up spiritual sacrifices acceptable to God** through Jesus Christ.* (1 Peter 2:5)

*For if by the one man's offense death reigned through the one, much more those who receive abundance of grace and of the gift of righteousness will **reign in life** through the One, Jesus Christ.*
(Romans 5:17)

As believers vested with Christ's imputed righteousness we have the responsibility to go before God in prayer and intercede for others. We are given special authority, as pertaining to our loved ones, to intercede for household salvation. Like Noah, we too may *"prepare an ark for the saving of [our] household"* (Hebrews 11:7) which is why he was counted as the eighth person saved from the flood, rather than the first (even though he was the head of his household):

*...and did not spare the ancient world – but preserved Noah, **the eighth man**, a herald of*

righteousness – crushing the world of the wicked by a downrush from above...

(2 Peter 2:5 Fenton)

Why did Peter refer to Noah as "the eighth man" or "the eighth person" (in other translations)? Could it be that Noah was the last of his loved ones to go into the ark? Genesis 7:16 says of the door of the ark that *"the LORD closed it behind him."*

Noah knew that he had found special favor in the eyes of the Lord and that, more than anything else, he wanted his family preserved from destruction. (*see* Genesis 6:8; Hebrews 11:7) Evidently, Noah purposed in his heart to not board the ark until all his loved ones had done so, knowing the Lord would not shut the door until he was safely inside. Even if this was not literally the case, the inspired record of Hebrews 11:7 says that his purpose in building the ark was to save his family.

Through intercessory prayer the believer can "prepare an ark," that is, a place of refuge, for his or her loved ones and can believe God, like Noah did, for the saving of his or her household. Like the Shunammite woman we can declare, *"it is well!"* even when our loved one is dead to the things of God. (*see* 2 Kings 4:26)

Intercession deals with the loved ones' faults before God, offering the merit of Jesus' blood on their behalf. God delivers them, even though they are not innocent, through the cleanness of our hands as we intercede for them. Of course, our cleanness is the righteousness of Christ that we have through faith in His blood. (*see* Romans 3:25)

As I was saying, the believer is not only a priest who offers spiritual sacrifices and stands in the gap for lost loved ones, but he or she is also a king who exercises authority over the enemy. Jesus gave us authority over all the power of the enemy, promising nothing shall by any means, or under any circumstances, hurt us. (*see* Luke 10:19) We can exercise authority, in the name of Jesus, over all the influences of Satan against our loved ones. As we will see in the next chapter, this is one of the primary reasons why the lost stay lost – they are under the influence of someone who hates them very much: the devil.

This is the essence of spiritual warfare. Intercession for our lost loved ones is directed God-ward (priestly ministry). Warfare is leveled against the enemy (kingly authority).

Jesus, the great High Priest, inaugurated, through the shedding of His blood, the new covenant when He sprinkled His blood on the mercy seat in the heavenly Holy of Holies (fulfilling the type of the ancient high priest on the Day of Atonement in Leviticus 16:23). When He sprinkled the blood He had previously shed He obtained an eternal redemption for us. He has made us priests unto God. Part of our priestly function is to offer up His blood in faith for the sins of others.

[At the end of the book I provide a prayer for your lost loved ones containing all the pertinent truths outlined in these pages. So don't bother yourself with trying to remember all these truths right now. Instead, let these truths soak into your heart and bring revelation into your spirit.]

3

How To Bind
The Mind Blinder

Who is the Mind Blinder?

*But even if our Gospel is veiled, it is veiled to those
who are perishing, whose minds the god of this age
has blinded, who do not believe lest the light of the
gospel of the glory of Christ, who is the image of
God, should shine on them.*

(2 Corinthians 4:3, 4)

No one would purposely drive over a cliff. He would
only do this if he was not in his right mind, or if he was
unable to see the impending danger. The Scriptures
teach that the lost are held in both conditions. Would
anyone in his right mind, clearly able to see eternal
values, reject Jesus Christ and refuse eternal life? Of
course not! The Gadarene was found sitting at Jesus'
feet, clothed, **and in his right mind** after his encounter
with the Nazarene. (*see* Mark 5:15) Before Jesus
delivered him he was of unsound mind. Who can
legitimately question that sin is not insanity?

Many millions are nearing death and approaching
judgment oblivious of their need to repent of their sins.
(*see* Hebrews 9:27) Underneath a multitutde of excuses
is a blinded reasoning.

The "mind blinder" has done his work!

Who is the mind blinder? Paul identifies him as *"the god of this age."* Jesus called him *"the ruler of this world," "the father of lies," "the devil," "a murderer from the beginning," "the evil one,"* and *"Beelzebub".* (*see* Matthew 6:13; Luke 11:18; John 8:44; 14:30)

The truly beautiful thing is that we have been given authority over all the ability of the one who blinds the minds of our loved ones!

It is important that when we attempt to share the Gospel with them that we do not get into an argumentative mode. When a lost loved one says, "I can't see what you're saying" believe him. He can't see. The god of this age has blinded his mind. *"Our wrestling match,"* Paul writes, *"is not against flesh and blood, but against the master-spirits of this dark world."* (Ephesians 6:12 Goodspeed)

The battle for your loved one's soul must be won in the spiritual realm.

Satan's Limitations

As believers we have authority, not over the will of the lost, but over Satan who blinds the minds of all unbelievers. We can bind "the mind blinder," permitting the glorious light of Jesus to shine upon the lost! Jesus gave us authority over *"all the power of the enemy."* (Luke 10:19) The Word gives us special authority, as discussed in chapters one and two, to intercede for blood relatives. **Believers can intercede to God for the salvation of their families with absolute confidence!** After we intercede, operating as priests on behalf of our families, we can violently attack the evil spirits holding sway over our loved ones' minds. This is partly what Jesus meant when He said, *"...the kingdom of heaven suffers violence, and the violent take it by force."* (Matthew 11:12) The Twentieth Century New Testament says *"men using force have been seizing it."* Jesus wants us to be forceful in taking that which He purchased for us by shedding and sprinkling His precious blood!

Jesus gave us authority over the devil, but we must exercise our authority in order for it to work. Don't be scared to exercise your authority! *"Resist the devil and he will flee from you."* (James 4:7b) If God told you to resist the devil you have an obligation to resist him. If God said the devil will flee from you, it means he will run from you as you stand against him in the mighty name of Jesus! Why not resist him on behalf of your loved one who is struggling under his controlling influence? You have authority in Christ to dominate the dominator, torment the tormentor, and victimize the victimizer! Let's look at Luke 10:19 more closely:

> *Behold, I give you the authority to trample on serpents and scorpions, and over all the power of the enemy, and nothing shall by any means hurt you.*

The word Jesus used for "authority" is the Greek word *exousia*. Vine's, Thayer's, Unger's, and a host of other lexical aids tell us that this word means privilege, authority, the right to rule or exercise authority, and to govern. Jesus gave His disciples the privilege and the right to exercise authority over all the power of the enemy!

The word Jesus used for "power" is the Greek word *dunamis*. The lexicons tell us that this word means the inherent ability of a thing or a person. Let me give one or two examples. The inherent ability, or *dunamis*, of an athlete can be measured by how far or fast he can run, how high he can jump, how much weight he can lift, etc. The inherent ability, or *dunamis*, of a car is measured by what is called "horsepower." The Bible teaches that Satan does have ability – indeed, much more ability than any human being. Yet his ability is limited. He is neither infinite nor is he omnipotent. He is finite and limited in his knowledge, his presence, and his power. While his knowledge, presence, and power are greater than any human being's, his functional attributes are limited. The Holy Spirit, on the other hand, is unlimited in His functional attributes, or inherent abilities. His *dunamis* is all powerful. Guess what? Not only has the believer been given authority over all of Satan's ability, but the very inherent ability of the Holy Spirit has been granted to the believer as well!

Our blessed Savior, just before He ascended, declared it!

> *And He said to them, "It is not for you to know times or seasons which the Father has put in His own authority. But you shall receive power when the Holy Spirit has come upon you;..."* (Acts 1:7, 8)

The word "power" is – you've guessed it – *dunamis*. Isn't this great! Our authority is greater than all of Satan's ability and our ability, through the Holy Spirit's anointing, is greater than all his ability too!

Many of God's children, however, are too timid to exercise their authority over the enemy. This is, itself, the influence of the devil over their unrenewed minds. Paul exhorted Timothy to be bold in his Lord and reminded him:

> *For God has not given us a spirit of timidity, but of power (dunamis) and love and discipline. Therefore do not be ashamed of the testimony of our Lord,...*
> (2 Timothy 1:7, 8a NASB)

Refuse timidity and embrace boldness! Boldly attack the devil. Engage in spiritual warfare. It is best to do this after you have spent some time in praise and worship of the Lord. Then, having the high praises of God in your mouth, and the two-edged sword of the Word in your hand, you can bind the devil's principalities and powers with the chains of Christ's authority and with the iron fetters of the Name of Jesus! (*see* Psalm 149:6, 8)

In order to bind the demon spirits working in the lives of your loved ones you must perceive which evil spirits are influencing them most. How can we perceive which evil spirits are holding sway over our loved ones' minds? By recognizing the fruit in their lives! Is your lost loved one filled with unbelief about Christ? Bind the spirit of unbelief in spiritual warfare. Is he bound by alcoholism or any other type of addiction? Bind the spirits of alcohol addiction, lust addiction, gambling addiction, etc. Here's how you do it: Vocally say, "I BIND THE SPIRIT OF _____ INFLUENCING MY LOVED ONE _____ (give his or her name). IN

THE NAME OF JESUS CHRIST YOU EVIL SPIRIT OF _____ MUST RELEASE _____ FROM YOUR INFLUENCE." (This information is included in the special prayer at the conclusion of the book.)

You may also pray for the gift of discerning of spirits (*see* 1 Corinthians 12:8-10) and believe for the Holy Spirit to reveal the specific identities of the evil spirits which are blinding the minds of your unsaved family members.

Binding the Strong Man

The truth we have been discussing is sometimes referred to as "binding the strong man." What does this term denote?

Jesus introduced this concept in Luke 11:21, 22 in the context of casting out demons.

> *When a strong man, fully armed, guards his own palace, his goods are in peace. But when a stronger than he comes upon him and overcomes him, he takes from him all his armor in which he trusted, and divides his spoils.*

Jesus is employing a parabolic metaphor which the people of His day readily understood. The "strong man" was Beelzebub, a common name for the devil which means "lord of the flies" (corruption). The devil, fully armed with all the weapons he uses against fallen human nature, guarded his palace (the world) and kept his goods (souls) in peace (free from threat of attack). That is, until Jesus came! Jesus is referring to Himself when He refers to someone who comes against the strong man who is *"stronger than he"* who *"overcomes him"* and *"takes from him all his armor in which he trusted"* (Satan's weapons of lies, fear, sickness, despair, etc.) and "divides his spoils" (rescues lost souls).

This is precisely what Jesus did at the Cross – He conquered Satan and all his hosts.

You might say, "This is well and good that Jesus defeated Satan, but how can this apply to my situation?" It applies in every way – simply put, you and I now rise up in the authority which our Conquering Lord has given us – authority which is greater than all of our enemy's ability – and bind him and his agents (demons) in the mighty Name above all names! This is what I referred to in the close of the previous chapter: spiritual warfare leveled against the devil, the very one who holds your unsaved loved one under his sway.

Jesus has made you a king! Exercise your authority over the evil one and watch his influence weaken and dissipate over the mind of the loved one for whom you are interceding. In fact, you as a kingdom warrior may bind what I call the "little strong man" (the demonic ruler who holds sway over your loved one). In most cases there is one principal spirit, above all others, which holds dominion over an unbeliever. Although the "strong man" in Jesus' teaching is obviously Satan, the "little strong man" is the strongest demon power over your loved ones' life. It may operate in the form of substance abuse (alcohol or drugs), or in a form of sinful behavior (sexual immorality or perversion, lying or stealing), or in a stronghold of the mind (psuedointellectualism, unbelief, gnosticism, liberalism, etc.).

The unseen realm is very real. It is more powerful than the seen realm and controls the seen realm. The Kingdom of God is much stronger than the domain of Satan, as will one day be clearly demonstrated in the seen realm. Until that happens we, as our King's regents upon the earth, can enforce the victory He won at the Cross when He spoiled principalities. (*see* Colossians 2:14,15)

It works! I've seen it work on behalf of my loved ones.

Uncle Jack Meets Jesus

When I was a young evangelist, still in my teens, one of my uncles, my father's brother Jack, came to visit us. Jack was a divorced alcoholic. His life was wasted and ruined. He felt he had sinned against the grace of God too much to ever be saved. (Jack had been raised in a strict holiness church in his youth which did not understand the free grace of God.)

I talked to Jack for hours during his visit with my father. Nothing I said seemed to penetrate the fog over his mind. During those early years of my ministry I spent many hours with God in prayer every day, divided in the early morning and late afternoon. One evening as I was returning from a period of glorious prayer, Uncle Jack was sitting on our front porch. I sensed the presence of the Lord very strongly upon my being but was unaware that Jack could tell it. He looked at me wide-eyed with astonishment. "What have you been doing?" he demanded. When I answered that I had been in prayer he replied that he had been around Christian people all his life but hadn't seen anyone's countenance so altered since he was a little boy and had seen his mother (my grandmother who deceased when my father was only four years of age) return from a "cottage prayer meeting," as they called it in those days.

"There's a simple explanation, Uncle," I responded, "God is real and He wants to be real to you too." With that I went on inside, leaving Jack alone with his thoughts.

The visit ended the next morning on a pleasant note. Uncle Jack was going home to south Texas that day and we all hugged him and said our good-byes.

About an hour later I was reading my Bible in the sanctuary of the church my father pastored, when the Holy Spirit prompted me to stop reading and start praying for Jack at that very instant. I obeyed. As I prayed I felt led to rebuke the powers of evil spirits and command them to leave Jack Alsobrook at that precise moment. Such glory and peace came over me! I announced it out loud in that empty auditorium: "Satan, you and your evil spirits release my uncle right now! In the Mighty Name of Jesus turn loose Jack Alsobrook's mind! Fog clear away!"

Later that night Jack called and told my father what had happened about an hour after he left our home. "I was heading south on Highway 287 when I pulled over on the side of the road and picked up a hitchhiker." "Oh, Jack," Dad responded, "you shouldn't be picking up hitchhikers! That can be dangerous." "Not this hitchhiker, Mack. It was the Lord Jesus Christ."

Jack went on to explain how he had pulled over to the side of the road because the Lord's presence had become so near and dear to him that he couldn't see to drive, and that he had invited Jesus to come into his heart. Dad asked, "Jack, what caused you to give your heart to Jesus at that particular time?" "Oh, I don't rightly know," Jack replied in his Texan drawl, "everything just became clear – all of a sudden – like a fog clearing before the sun."

I believe that my prayer was precisely timed by the Holy Spirit and that my word of rebuke caused the evil one to release his influence over my uncle's mind. As Jack's thoughts cleared he could understand the plan of salvation, clear and simple, and was able to receive the Lord Jesus into his heart without any demonic interference.

I am happy to tell you that Jack served the Lord for the next two years, studying his Bible faithfully and telling anyone who would listen to him the wondrous story of Jesus. One night Jack passed away sweetly in his sleep, with a smile on his face. I look forward to seeing him again!

Standing in Faith

Jack's salvation occurred very quickly. I had begun praying for him earnestly a few days before his conversion, when he first came to visit us, and was commanding Satan to loose him at the very moment Jack opened his heart to Jesus. It surely didn't take long! But another relative I prayed for took three years to come to the Lord. During this interval she appeared to become even worse.

This can be discouraging to the intercessor. But we

must continue to stand in the gap and make up the hedge for our loved one, otherwise our faith will be hindered from believing for the power of God unto our loved ones' salvation. We cannot be moved by their present state of spiritual death. A faith-filled Christian is someone who, like the heroes in the Faith Hall of Fame, does not take things at face value, but *"endures by seeing Him who is invisible."* (Hebrews 11:27) Keep praying, believing, and standing in faith for that loved one. *"Do not cast away your confidence which has great reward."* (Hebrews 10:35)

We are given a beautiful example of this in the Scriptures. A story of someone who was not moved by the present appearance of death in her child. It is an Old Testament story, which Paul says, is an example to us today. (*see* Romans 15:4) Whereas the Shunnamite's story is focused in the natural realm, our faith applies it, as the new covenant does all the old covenant, to the spiritual realm. (*see* Hebrews 10:1)

"It Is Well"

The Shunammite woman in the Old Testament is an example of an intercessor who dared to believe for life in the very face of death.

Her story begins with Elisha, the famous prophet who passed by her home frequently on his circuit. This woman and her husband noted the journeys of the man of God and thought to do him a kindness. They built a room, what we term today "a prophet's chamber," so the prophet would have a private rest area available to him whenever he needed it. (*see* 2 Kings 4)

One day, while Elisha was resting in his special room, he turned to his servant, Gehazi, and asked him what favor, or blessing, had they bestowed upon the couple in return for their favor. This principle of blessing those who bless the servants of God was elucidated centuries later by our Lord Jesus Christ: *"He who receives a prophet in the name of a prophet shall receive a prophet's reward..."* (Matthew 10:41)

Gehazi called the Shunammite to the chamber and Elisha asked her what blessing would she like to receive in return for all she had done for him. She replied that she and her husband had no unmet needs. Gehazi then observed that the couple was childless. "Very well, then," Elisha prophesied, "about this time I will return next year and you shall be embracing a son." The very next year her little bundle of joy arrived. She received her reward in the form of a much desired child!

For thirteen years the Shunammite couple enjoyed their "reward." It isn't difficult to imagine the joy this little fellow brought to their quiet home. One day tragedy struck when the boy, now a teenager, was out in the field with his father. *"My head, my head,"* he cried out in pain while collapsing on the ground. A servant carried him to his mother, where *"he sat on her knees until noon, and then died."*

It is precisely here that the mother displayed her tremendous strength of spirit. Without informing her husband of the son's death, she asked him to provide a donkey and a servant so she could go to the man of God. *"Why?"* he asked, *"it is neither new moon or sabbath."* She responded, *"it shall be well,"* and rode off.

As she was nearing Mount Carmel, the man of God

noticed her from afar and ordered Gehazi to run out and specifically ask her if all was well with her family. *"It is well,"* she replied. Then, when she reached Elisha, she fell at his feet and poured out her soul. Prostrate before the man of God she acknowledged that the boy was dead (which is a perfect type of intercessory faith). To condense the rest of the story, suffice it to say that the boy was raised from the dead. But the important point for us to notice is her response, first to her husband, and then to the prophet's servant: ***It is well.*** The Shunammite woman was operating on the principle of Romans 4:17 which teaches us to be like God and call those things that be not as though they were:

> *...in the presence of Him whom he (Abraham) believed – God, who gives life to the dead and calls those things which do not exist as though they did;...*

Jesus taught that His followers are to operate on this same principle:

> *Now in the morning, as they passed by, they saw the fig tree dried up from the roots. And Peter, remembering, said to Him, "Rabbi, look! The fig tree which You cursed has withered away."*

> *So Jesus answered and said to them, "Have faith in God. For assuredly, I say to you, whoever says to this mountain, 'Be removed and be cast into the sea,' and does not doubt in his heart, but believes that those things he says will be done, he will have whatever he says. Therefore I say to you, whatever*

things you ask when you pray, believe that you receive them, and you will have them.

(Mark 11:20-24)

When Jesus cursed the fig tree it was in full bloom. It took a day for it to wither in the seen realm, which Peter called to mind the following morning. Jesus used this as an example for us to follow. We are to believe that those things which we say about our loved ones will be done and are to believe that we receive the answer to our prayers even before we have them. We are to believe we receive whatever we are asking for when we ask for it. *"Receive it when you are praying and you will have it later,"* Jesus is teaching in Mark 11:24.

Special Promises for Parents

The response most parents give about their erring children is quite opposite to this ancient woman of faith. Countless times I have heard distraught parents sigh, "My son is in the night clubs; my daughter is on drugs. I raised them up right. Why has God let this happen? I'm afraid both my children will end up in hell." It may not be a lack of faith to confide this to a minister who will stand in the gap through intercessory prayer, however, this is the same thing many troubled parents tell anyone who will listen. I understand that no one can worry you like a child, one's own flesh and blood, but all this type of talk does is hinder faith on the part of the parents and can even discourage someone who desires to help through intercession. The proper response is: **It is well.** This is the language of believing faith. The concerned parent has every right to cast his or her concerns over on the Lord through intercessory prayer and make a strong stand in faith for one's children. (*see* 1 Peter 5:7)

The interceding parent can boldly proclaim, **"all my children shall be the Lord's disciples and shall have great peace!"** because God promises...

> *All your children shall be taught by the LORD, and great shall be the peace of your children.*
>
> (Isaiah 54:13)

Parents of unbelieving children should comfort their hearts during the interval between their intercession and warfare on behalf of their erring children and the salvation for which they are believing with these words from the prophet Jeremiah:

> *Thus says the LORD: Refrain your voice from weeping and your eyes from tears; for your work shall be rewarded, says the LORD; and they shall come again from the land of the enemy. There is hope in your future, says the LORD, that your children shall come back to their own border.*
>
> (Jeremiah 31:16, 17)

Let me remind you of this truth: When Jesus ratified the new covenant, He sprinkled His blood on the Mercy Seat in the heavenly Holy of Holies and obtained an **eternal redemption** for us. (*see* Hebrews 9:12) In doing so, Jesus made everyone who believes upon Him both a king and a priest. **A king governs:** *"Where the* *word of a king is, there is power."* (Ecclesiastes 8:4) **A priest offers sacrifices:** *"Every priest... offers sacrifices for sin."* (Hebrews 5:1).

How It Works

As a priest, the believer can go before God and offer the Blood of Jesus on behalf of his children. As a king, the believer can bind the mind blinder (Satan) through the authority of Christ. By binding the devil away from his children, the influence of Satan over the believer's family is rendered null and void. This opens the children up to the gentle influences of the Holy Spirit, the great Helper, who came to convict of sin, righteousness, and judgment. (*see* John 16:8) A young person, thus freed from satanic influence and under the Spirit's dealings, will naturally choose the One who is "altogether lovely" over the one who *"comes to steal, to kill, and to destroy."* (Song of Songs 5:16; John 10:10)

The mind blinder can be bound and the captive can be set free!

4

Instructions For Using
The Special Prayer

On the pages which follow you will find the special prayer I have referred to throughout this book.

Before lifting up this prayer, feel free to photocopy it so you can insert the names of all your lost loved ones, one by one, and keep the photocopied sheets as reminders and prayer contacts. You may want to lay your hand upon these prayer sheets from time to time.

You may also write me and send the names of all your loved ones for whom you are praying. I will stand in agreement with you, as I have for hundreds of others, for their salvation.

A Special Intercession For
My Loved One's Salvation

Heavenly Father, as a member of the New Covenant priesthood, I now come to You through Jesus Christ who is the High Priest of my confession.

I approach You not for myself but on the behalf of _____my loved one whose mind has been blinded by the ruler of this age.

Holy Father, I come to You in _____'s stead requesting that You grant mercy and favor to (him/her). (He/she) is not innocent, but because of the efficacy of the Cross, I ask You to wash away (his/her) sins with the power of the precious blood of Christ. Father, I realize (he/she) will need to come to You and request this same thing of (his/her) own volition, but I ask it in faith and believe there is a hedge of divine protection around (him/her) right now through the Blood. I acknowledge the merits of the Blood for my loved one, _____.

As a new covenant priest, I take (his/her) place before You, standing in the gap for _____. Furthermore, I ask that (he/she) will be delivered from the dominion of darkness and translated into the kingdom of Your dear Son. I am reminded of Your promise to deliver the one for whom I intercede who is not innocent, and this one for whom I intercede shall be delivered through the cleanness of my hands. Like Abraham who besought You on Lot's behalf, I beseech You on _____'s behalf. Jesus has made me both a king and a priest. I lift up my loved one to you as a member of the royal priesthood. I take my stand against Satan as a king under the headship of the King of Kings.

Satan, before the face of God, I take my stand against you in the Mighty Name of Jesus Christ and refuse to allow you, the enemy, to kill or destroy _____. I declare, by faith, that you, the mind blinder are bound, and that your influence is broken in the life of _____. I specifically bind spirits of _____ in the Name of the Lord Jesus Christ. No longer will my loved one, _____, live under a fog of demonic influence, but (his/her) mind is free and clear, able to respond to the convicting power of the Holy Spirit. I bind all spirits of _____ influencing my loved one. In the name of Jesus Christ you evil spirit of _____ must release _____ from your influence!

Just as Lazarus was raised from death to new life, I come to You on behalf of _____ and ask that You raise (him/her) from spiritual death to eternal life. I thank you, Father, that soon (he/she) will come forth into newness of life. (He/she) will come out of darkness and into light, out of sin and into righteousness, out of rebellion and into submission, out of hardness and into tenderness for the Son of God who loved (him/her) and gave Himself for (him/her).

I thank you, Lord Jesus, that the true light of your love is now shining upon _____.

I ask You to send forth laborers to lead (him/her) to salvation.

Father I put You in remembrance and plead my case, in Jesus' name. You have promised, "Believe in the Lord Jesus Christ, and you shall be saved, and your house." My loved one, _____, therefore is saved by faith and I accept no other outcome.

IN THE HOLY NAME OF JESUS CHRIST, MY LORD AND SAVIOR, I PRAY AND BELIEVE!

Amen.

_____

(Your Name)

About the Author

DAVID ALSOBROOK was a minister's son but chose to rebel against the church's teachings at an early age. He studied karate and false religions before committing his life to Jesus Christ at the age of 15. Before his sixteenth birthday he had read the entire Bible through four times and discovered, to his great joy, that the truths which his church taught were no longer in effect still were and are available to believers today.

At the age of 17, David entered full-time traveling ministry in early '72 majoring in evangelism and Bible teaching. He has traveled the United States and Canada extensively and has preached in more than 1,200 different places, from jails to country clubs, from a handful of people to thousands at a time. He has written over forty books which have been distributed to approximately fifty nations, having been translated in no fewer than fifteen languages. Conservative estimates of his press runs exceed four million copies. Noted leaders of the Christian community have quoted largely from his material in their publications.

The half million copies of his book on abortion, placed in many counseling centers across the U.S. and Canada, has resulted in numerous young mothers deciding to birth their babies rather than abort them. People from all walks of life, from prisoners to presidents, have read and commented favorably on his writings and the lives of many people in many parts of the world have been forever changed by the power of the Word of God as testified in the thousands of grateful letters David has received from more than forty nations.

If you have enjoyed this book and would like to help us to send a copy of it and many other titles to needy pastors in the **Third World**, please write for further information or send your gift to:

Sovereign World Trust, P.O. Box 777, Tonbridge, Kent TN11 0ZS, United Kingdom

or to the **'Sovereign World'** distributor in your country.